CELLS
AND
DISEASE

Barbara A. Somervill

Heinemann
LIBRARY
Chicago, Illinois

www.heinemannraintree.com
Visit our website to find out
more information about
Heinemann-Raintree books.

To order:
☎ Phone 888-454-2279
🖥 Visit www.heinemannraintree.com
to browse our catalog and order online.

Edited by Megan Cotugno and Andrew Farrow
Designed by Philippa Jenkins
Original illustrations © Capstone Global Library, Ltd.
Illustrated by KJA-artists.com
Picture research by Hannah Taylor
Production by Alison Parsons
Originated by Capstone Global Library, Ltd.
Printed by Leo Paper Products, Ltd.

14 13 12 11 10
10 9 8 7 6 5 4 3 2 1

Library of Congress Cataloging-in-Publication Data
Somervill, Barbara A.
  Cells and disease / Barbara A. Somervill.
    p. cm. -- (Investigating cells)
  Includes bibliographical references and index.
  ISBN 978-1-4329-3881-9 (hc)
  1. Cells--Juvenile literature. 2. Bacteria--Juvenile
literature. 3. Diseases--Juvenile literature. I. Title.
  QH582.5.S663 2011
  571.9--dc22
                              2009049981

Acknowledgments
The author and publishers are grateful to the
following for permission to reproduce copyright
material: ©Alamy Images pp. 11 (©PHOTOTAKE/
Scott Bodell), 21 (©moodboard), 24 (©Nigel
Cattlin); ©Corbis pp. 6 (Simon Jarratt), 8 (Dennis
Kunkel Microscopy, Inc./Visuals Unlimited), 15
(Bettmann); ©istockphoto pp. 22 (©Judith Bicking),
30 (©Monkey Business Images/Catherine Yeulet),
31 (©Freeze Frame Studio); ©Photolibrary pp.
4 (Rick Gomez), 9 (Image 100), 19 (Roger Eritja),
23 (Erproductions, Ltd.), 25 (Claire Higgins), 36
(Heiner Heine), 37 (Javier Larrea), 38 (Astier),
42 (Huntstock); ©Science Photo Library pp. 5
(Susumu Nishinaga), 7, 10 (Cristina Pedrazzini),
13 (David McCarthy), 16 (M. Wurtz/Biozentrum,
University of Basel), 18 (Scott Camazine), 27 (Debra
Ferguson/AgstockUSA), 29 (Sheila Terry), 32 (Steve
Gschmeissner), 34 (Simon Fraser), 35 (AMI Images),
43 (Suzanne Grala); ©shutterstock p. 40 (©vadim
kozlovsky).

Cover photograph of Asian flu viruses reproduced
with the permission of Science Photo Library (Dr. R.
Dourmashkin).

We would like to thank Michelle Raabe, Ph.D., for
her invaluable help in the preparation of this book.

Every effort has been made to contact copyright
holders of any material reproduced in this book. Any
omissions will be rectified in subsequent printings if
notice is given to the publisher.

Disclaimer
All the Internet addresses (URLs) given in this book
were valid at the time of going to press. However,
due to the dynamic nature of the Internet, some
addresses may have changed, or sites may have
changed or ceased to exist since publication. While
the author and publisher regret any inconvenience
this may cause readers, no responsibility for any
such changes can be accepted by either the author
or the publisher.

Contents

Some words are printed in bold, **like this**. You can find out what they mean by looking in the glossary.

What Is a Cell?

What do a cactus, a swan, and a person all have in common? They are all **organisms** (living things) that are made up of cells, the smallest units of life.

When these organisms are healthy, their life processes run smoothly. They take in **nutrients**, the substances that help the body grow and stay healthy. They rid themselves of waste. They grow and move. They are sensitive to hot and cold, and to light and darkness. They may eventually produce young. These are all important life processes.

Got cells?

The human body has more than 200 different types of cells. Each kind of cell does a particular job. For example, there are three different types of bone cell in human bodies. Muscle cells help bodies move. Blood cells carry oxygen and nutrients to other cells throughout the body.

During exercise, cells may work more quickly. This is because the body needs oxygen faster. The body also produces more cell waste, starts to sweat, and so on.

When healthy people exercise, cells work hard to move oxygen through the body and remove carbon dioxide waste.

How small are cells?

Cells come in many shapes and sizes, but most cannot be seen with the eye alone. Cells are so small that they are measured in microns. A micron is equal to one-millionth of a meter. The period at the end of this sentence is gigantic compared to the size of a cell. When you become an adult, your body will have between 50 trillion and 100 trillion cells. A trillion is a million million!

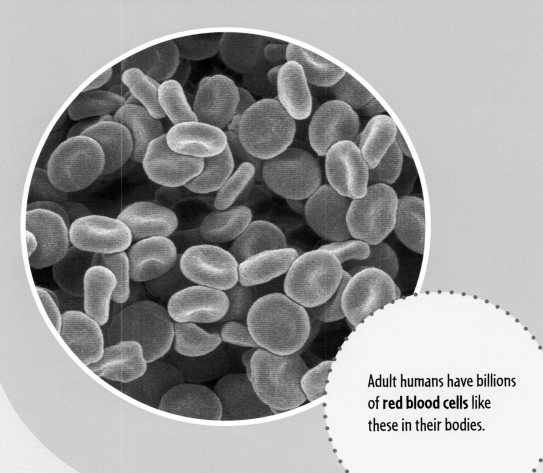

Adult humans have billions of **red blood cells** like these in their bodies.

How do cells work like the human body?

Cells work a lot like the human body. For example, on average throughout your lifetime, about 60 percent of your body is made up of water. Your body takes in nutrients, and this water carries the nutrients throughout your body. Similarly, your cells are made up of at least 70 percent water. Cells turn vitamins, **minerals**, sugars, **fats** (substances that store energy), and **proteins** (substances that build tissues) into usable products. They build stronger bones and muscles, in addition to giving you energy.

Your body gets rid of waste products through **urine** (liquid waste) and **feces** (solid waste). When cells have used up nutrients, they also make waste. Cell waste can be broken proteins or dead cells. Getting rid of waste is a normal life process.

Disease and life processes

Unfortunately, all organisms can get sick. When that happens, disease affects an organism's cells and upsets its life processes. Disease changes how the body deals with a normal day's work.

This woman is suffering from cancer, a disease that affects a person's cells.

When disease strikes, some kinds of cells go to war to get rid of the invaders. To help the cells win against invading disease, humans need to eat the right foods, drink plenty of liquids, and get enough rest. Cells will then have a better chance of successfully fighting disease.

Scientist Spotlight

Antony van Leeuwenhoek

In the 1600s, studying science was something only wealthy men could afford to do. Holland's Antony van Leeuwenhoek (1632–1723) was not wealthy, but he was determined. He educated himself and became an expert in biology. As he studied, he made more than 500 microscopes to help his studies. The microscopes were crude compared to today's microscopes, but they were amazing for the time and met Leeuwenhoek's needs. Using his homemade instruments, Leeuwenhoek became the first person to identify **bacteria**, **protists** (a kind of tiny organism), blood cells, and many other microscopic living things.

Leeuwenhoek was the first scientist to identify bacteria.

How Does Illness Affect My Cells?

You have a headache and a high fever. Your muscles and joints ache. Or maybe your skin has broken out in a rash, and the itch is driving you crazy. What is going on?

A disease is any problem that prevents the body from functioning normally. Humans can get sick from many different **agents**. An **infection** is when the presence of **bacteria**, a **virus**, or another agent causes disease.

Infections caused by bacteria and viruses lead to fevers, **vomiting**, aches and pains, and rashes. Infections caused by a **fungus** may attack skin cells, making them itch and burn. **Parasites** are foreign creatures that feed on blood or **tissues**.

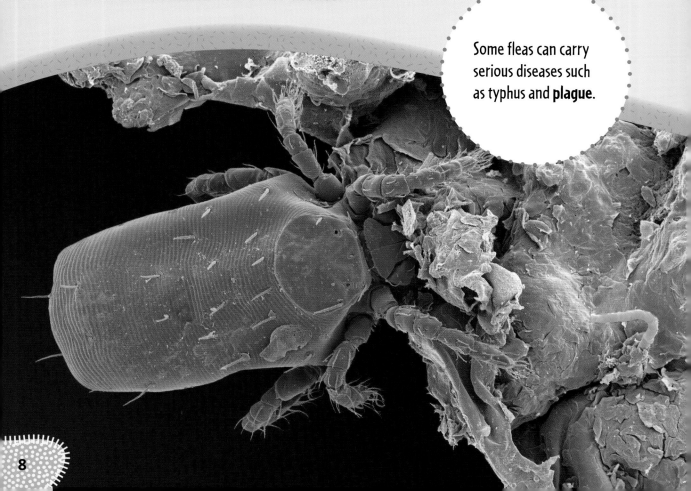

Some fleas can carry serious diseases such as typhus and **plague**.

When you are sick with a fever, your body needs rest so the cells can fight the disease.

What happens when you get sick?

When you become sick, your cells have to work extremely hard to help heal you. If there is some type of infection, **white blood cells** rush to the place where the infection is hiding. **Lymph** organs, including lymph **nodes**, tonsils, the spleen, and the thymus, contain white blood cells. These lymph organs respond to infection by reproducing cells rapidly. As a result, the areas under your arms, where lymph nodes are located, swell and feel sore.

Other kinds of cells are also affected by an infection. For example, nerve cells carry messages throughout your body. They tell the brain where your body hurts or itches. Other cells produce a slimy substance called **mucus** that blocks your nose and throat. This makes it harder for you to breathe, so other cells struggle to get enough oxygen.

If you vomit (throw up), you take in less food and water. Your cells have to work with less fuel. You feel tired. Your cells need you to sleep so that they can have a chance to fight your disease. Sleep requires you to use less energy and allows your cells to regenerate, or restore themselves.

How do doctors identify diseases?

Some diseases show themselves in obvious ways, such as fevers, a runny nose, vomiting, or rashes. These are called **symptoms**. Diseases with obvious signs include flu, colds, and chicken pox. Those signs show that your cells have found and are fighting the invaders. Symptoms are similar to signs. They include things that the infected person feels, but might not be easily measured by a doctor—for example, a headache.

Other diseases have signs and symptoms that are not quite so obvious. Identifying these diseases may require blood, **urine**, or other medical tests. Urine tests show how much sugar, **protein**, or bacteria may be in the urine.

A blood test shows levels of **red blood cells** and white blood cells, and if the blood is carrying an infection.

Can other agents cause diseases in cells?

Not all diseases are caused by foreign invaders. These other diseases are often called **disorders** or conditions. Some disorders may be **inherited**, meaning they are passed down from parents. Sickle-cell anemia, Tay-Sachs, and cystic fibrosis are passed on from parent to child through something called **deoxyribonucleic acid (DNA)**. DNA carries the traits and characteristics of a living thing. It makes up units of information called **genes**. Inherited diseases are called **genetic** diseases, because they are related to genes. (See pages 38–40 for more on genetic diseases.)

Other medical conditions are caused by environmental problems, such as poisoning and exposure to **radiation**. Radiation are bits of energy that can cause changes to cell structures. People exposed to radiation may not only become sick, they can also have their DNA damaged or develop cancer. If they live, genetic **mutations** (changes in genes) can be passed on to their children.

Even common injuries can be serious dangers. For example, some people are highly allergic to poison ivy, dust, and mold. Some people can even die after a bee sting. Poison ivy, bee stings, and allergies make people sick and may require a doctor's care.

DNA carries the traits and characteristics of a living thing. Its shape is called a double helix. It looks like a twisted rope ladder.

What Are Bacteria?

Bacteria belong to the kingdom called Monera. They are very simple, one-celled **organisms**. Bacteria do not have organelles, which are the working parts of all other plant and animal cells. A single bacterium does not have an organized nucleus, which is the command center for other cells.

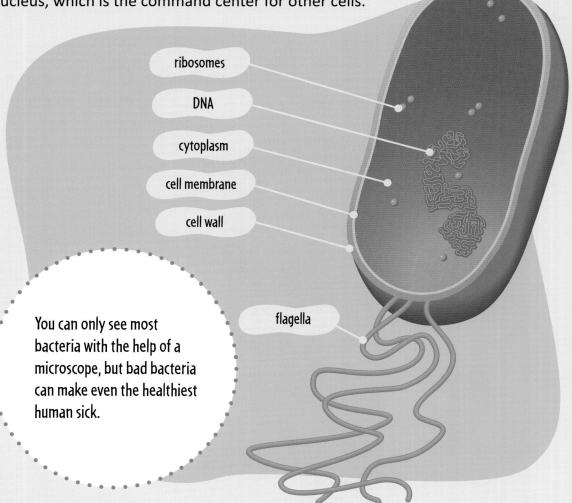

ribosomes

DNA

cytoplasm

cell membrane

cell wall

flagella

You can only see most bacteria with the help of a microscope, but bad bacteria can make even the healthiest human sick.

There are thousands of known types of bacteria, and many kinds of bacteria live in your body. Average adult humans have 10 times as many bacteria in their bodies as they have human cells. Don't worry—most bacteria in your body are "good" bacteria. Without them, you could not digest food.

Bad bacteria

But not all bacteria are good bacteria. Some bacteria cause diseases, such as typhoid fever or cholera. Bacteria enter the body in many different ways. They can be carried in the air and breathed into the lungs. Tuberculosis and strep throat are caused by bacteria that are transported by sneezing, coughing, and even talking.

Bacteria may live in food and be eaten. Salmonella and Listeria, two types of bacteria-based food poisoning, are bacteria carried in food. Bacteria can pass from one person to another by physical contact, such as through a handshake or a hug.

Animals may also carry bacteria. Such animals are called **vectors**. Fleas, for example, were vectors for the bubonic **plague**, also called the black death. The disease killed more than 25 million people between 1347 and 1352.

Science tools: the microscope

In 1590 Dutch eyeglass makers Zacharias and Hans Jansen made the first microscope. It was a tube with glass lenses at each end. Today's microscopes work like the Jansens' microscope, but are much more powerful. They have an upper lens (at the eyepiece) and lenses below. A powerful microscope is needed to see **viruses** and bacteria.

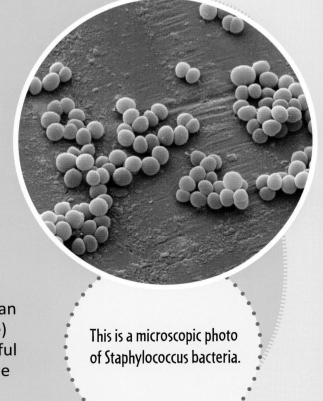

This is a microscopic photo of Staphylococcus bacteria.

Infection

Once bacteria enter the body, **infection** begins. The bacteria begin to rapidly reproduce. A microscopic battle begins. **White blood cells**, which are part of the blood, race to attack the bacteria. If there are few bacteria, the white cells win, and the bacteria will die. If the bacteria reproduce quickly enough, they cause disease.

Even though the bacteria have succeeded in causing a disease, the body's **immune system** (the system that fights disease and illness) will continue to fight. In the meantime, the disease may cause much damage. Disease-causing bacteria may produce toxins, or poisons, that cause muscle cramps, **vomiting**, or **paralysis** (the inability to move muscles). You may develop a fever, vomiting, **diarrhea** (runny or liquid **feces**), or heavy **mucus**. Most of your normal life processes do not function well while the disease rages in your body. You feel the need to sleep a lot, which gives your cells a chance to fight the infection.

Bacteria fight back

Before 1928 there was no efficient medicine for fighting a bacterial infection. In that year, Sir Alexander Fleming discovered penicillin, the first **antibiotic**. An antibiotic destroys bacteria. Today we have a wide range of antibiotics, and most are effective in curing disease.

Bacteria, like all living things, want to survive. Even though people have created more powerful antibiotics, there continue to be new kinds of powerful bacteria as well. The bacteria that cause tuberculosis, a disease that used to be cured with penicillin, have changed to develop a resistance to antibiotics, making it more difficult to cure a patient with tuberculosis.

Scientist Spotlight

Alexander Fleming

Scottish doctor, researcher, and Nobel Prize–winner Alexander Fleming (1881–1955) investigated the source of various types of infections. He discovered that bacteria caused most infections and looked for a way to kill the bacteria. Fleming found that a substance created by a type of mold was a good bacteria killer. From this, he developed penicillin in 1928. Penicillin did not become widely available, however, until the 1940s. Penicillin was the first effective antibiotic, and it is still used today.

Fleming's work opened the door for the discovery of many different antibiotics.

What Is a Virus?

It is easier to explain what a **virus** is not than to say what it is. A virus is not a plant or an animal. It is not a cell. It cannot live on its own.

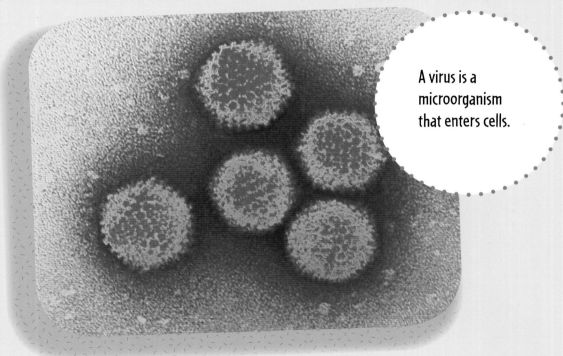

A virus is a microorganism that enters cells.

Viruses are **microorganisms** (very tiny living things), smaller than **bacteria**, that invade living cells and cause disease. Viruses are **parasites**, much like head lice or leeches, but they survive inside cells. They can be made up of **deoxyribonucleic acid (DNA)** or **ribonucleic acid (RNA)** (which sends instructions to cells), wrapped up in a layer of **protein**. Cells already contain protein and nucleic acid. As a result, viruses settle in easily. They find a cell to invade and become part of that cell.

An invaded **organism** is called a **host**. Because a virus cannot survive without a host, it might seem that there is no way for viruses to move from person to person. However, viruses are crafty. They can hang around on glasses, door handles, or pillowcases and wait for a host to come along. If a person drinks out of a glass that has a virus on it, the virus enters the body and invades a cell. The virus takes over the machinery of the host cell and forces it to make more viruses.

What is a cold?

Your nose runs. Your head aches. Your throat is sore. Most people get at least one cold a year. Unfortunately, there is no cure. More than 200 different viruses cause colds. A cold virus invades the cells in the nose and throat. The cells react, sending a message that they need protection. That protection is **mucus**. Increased mucus production traps a virus, and coughing and sneezing help to remove it from the body. The only solution for a cold is to let it run its course.

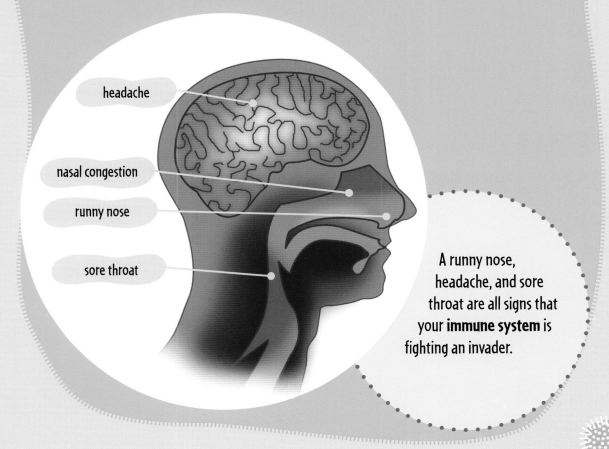

headache

nasal congestion

runny nose

sore throat

A runny nose, headache, and sore throat are all signs that your **immune system** is fighting an invader.

What can be done to control disease-causing viruses?

Viral **infections** are difficult to treat. This is because the majority of the virus is hiding inside host cells, out of reach of the immune system. Scientists are working to find cures for viral diseases. But it is difficult to develop medicines that destroy viruses without killing normal human cells.

Scientists have, however, developed a number of **vaccines** for viral diseases. Vaccines prevent a person from getting a disease, or at least reduce the effects of the disease. Vaccines are effective against smallpox, chicken pox, and flu. While smallpox vaccine prevents the disease, flu vaccines do not always work against a specific flu. A flu vaccine is effective against the flu virus it was made from. Flu viruses change so quickly that vaccines may only be partly effective.

Some animals and insects carry viruses to humans and other animals. They are called **vectors**. Mosquitoes, ticks, and lice are common insect vectors. They deliver the virus into the blood of any animal they bite. Larger animals, such as pigs, dogs, or fish, can also be vectors.

Chicken pox is not seen as often today as it once was in the United States. This is because many children are vaccinated against this virus.

Chicken soup for your cells

In 1993 scientists at the University of Nebraska Medical Center scientifically proved what mothers have known for centuries. The scientists tested 13 store-bought chicken soups and one homemade chicken soup. They found that all the soups helped relieve cold signs and **symptoms**. Colds and flu increase mucus in the body, which produces runny noses and wheezing coughs. Chicken soup reduces mucus production. The nose clears, coughing decreases, and patients feel better. The next time you feel sick, try some chicken soup. It works!

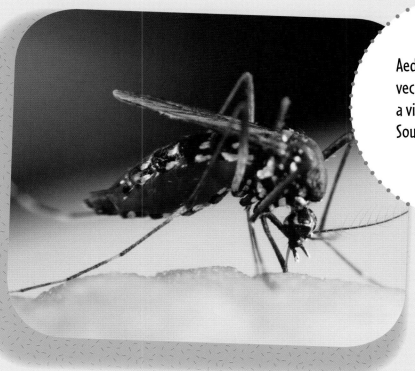

Aedes mosquitoes are the vectors for yellow fever, a viral disease found in South America and Africa.

How Do Our Cells Fight Disease?

As soon as your body senses an invader, your cells begin to fight back. In the battle for good health, your body sends its best warriors.

Whether the disease wins or your defending cells win depends on many conditions. Invading agents attack your body every day. Most of the time, your cells defeat them, and you do not get sick. When you do get sick, do not think your cells have given up. Cells in your **immune system** do not quit easily.

Lymph at work

To be **immune** to something means to be protected from that specific disease-causing agent. Your body protects itself through a system of **tissues**, cells, and organs. When invaders get into the body, a clear liquid called **lymph** carries them to lymphatic organs, mainly the lymph **nodes**. These nodes act like a disease filter. They filter out **viruses**, **bacteria**, and **fungi** to help your body avoid sickness. Inside the lymph nodes are **white blood cells** that look for invaders and then mount an immune response.

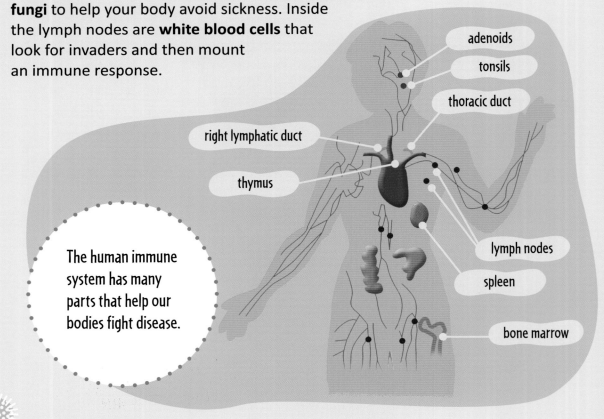

adenoids

tonsils

thoracic duct

right lymphatic duct

thymus

lymph nodes

spleen

bone marrow

The human immune system has many parts that help our bodies fight disease.

Flu often begins with a runny nose, coughing, and itchy eyes.

How does the immune system work?

Let's look at how the immune system works in different situations. Let's say that when you go to bed, you have a stuffy nose, sore throat, and itchy eyes. You wake up with a fever, headache, and aching joints. You have the flu.

What are your cells doing about it? Lymph nodes swell and become painful as the nodes try to filter virus-infected cells and free-floating virus from your body. **Bone marrow** (substance inside bones) produces extra white blood cells to hunt for and destroy infected cells. It may take several days or even weeks for your immune system to beat the virus.

An instant reaction

Say you fall down and skin your knee. You have broken through your first layer of defense against disease— your skin. Millions of cells instantly go to work.

Your body sees a cut in the skin as an attack. This is because dirt and other debris can get into the cut. White blood cells and platelets rush to the wound. The platelets are the part of the blood that form a clot to prevent blood from leaking out, and more germs from sneaking in. The clot forms a scab. Inside your body, white blood cells attack any germs that entered the body.

Get vaccinated

As a child, you may have been vaccinated against several different diseases. When you are vaccinated, your blood cells produce special **proteins** called antibodies. Antibodies are made in response to an invader.

You need a different antibody for measles than for chicken pox or mumps. **Vaccines** produce memory cells. If you come into contact with that invader again, the cells are ready to attack it. Other vaccines, like tetanus vaccine, only work for a few years. These vaccines launch a milder immune response and less memory is produced. These vaccines require "boosters" to keep your immunity up.

When your skin is cut, white blood cells race to the area to fight against **infection**.

Scientist Spotlight

Edward Jenner

The scientist who developed the first effective vaccine was Englishman Edward Jenner (1749–1823). In Jenner's time, smallpox was a certain killer. Jenner noticed that dairy workers who suffered from cowpox, a disease less deadly than smallpox, never got smallpox.

In 1796 Jenner took cowpox fluid from a dairymaid and gave an eight-year-old boy cowpox. The boy got mildly sick. Seven weeks later, Jenner tried to give the same boy smallpox, but the boy did not get sick. Jenner decided to call this new procedure vaccination—from the Latin word for cow, *vacca*, and the name of the cowpox virus, *vaccinia*. Today, smallpox no longer threatens lives, thanks to Jenner's discovery.

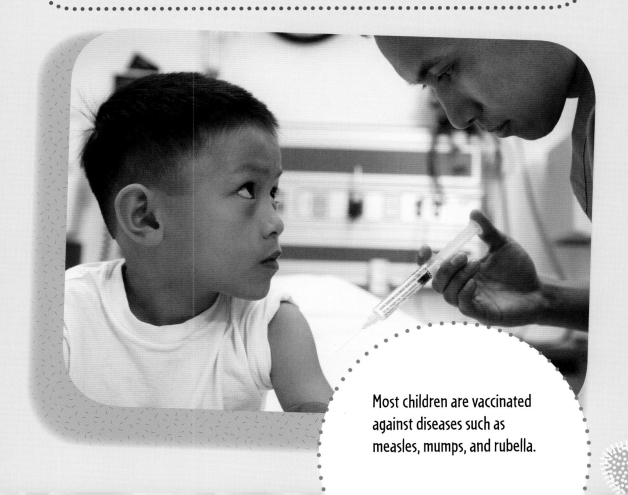

Most children are vaccinated against diseases such as measles, mumps, and rubella.

Can Plants Get Sick?

When plants get sick, there is no way to take their temperatures or feed them chicken soup. Plant disease is any condition that stops plants from growing normally or producing fruit.

With plants that provide food, such as wheat or corn, the loss of a crop from disease can be serious. Humans and animals go hungry. With plants normally sold to gardeners, a sick-looking plant cannot be sold. This hurts the business of the plant seller. If a sick plant does get sold, it can spread disease to other plants.

What causes plant sickness?

Fungi, **bacteria**, and **viruses** make plants sick, just as they make people sick. Plants also get sick from too much or too little water, too few **minerals** in the soil, and **pollution** (harmful substances in the air and water). Heat, insects, and lightning play roles in plant sickness as well.

This potato looks as though it has been burned, but it actually has a bacterial **infection** that makes potatoes rot.

Plants do not have the same **symptoms** of illness as people or animals. Typical signs of a sick plant include shriveled leaves, small fruit, or rot, which is cell death and decay. Plants may also have blotches, blight, canker, and galls. Blotches are spots on leaves. Blight makes leaves dry up or shrivel. Canker develops a dry, dead section on a plant's stem or a tree's trunk. Galls are large growths on a plant, usually on a stem, branch, or trunk.

Canker forms dead bark. There will be no new growth on this tree if the canker is severe and affects the main trunk of the tree.

The right conditions

A plant needs four conditions for it to become sick:

- First, the plant must be the right **host** for a disease. Some diseases only attack tobacco, while others attack only roses or only cucumber vines, for example.

- Second, the environment must support the disease. It cannot be too hot, cold, dry, or wet.

- Third, a virus, bacterium, or fungus must be on the plant or in the soil.

- Fourth, the **agent** must have enough time to take over the plant.

How do plant cells respond to disease?

When disease attacks animals or humans, their **immune systems** fight the disease. Plants also have a type of immune system that fights disease so that they can survive. In plants, war against disease is a chemical war.

When a disease attacks a plant, the plant's cells detect the invader. The plant produces a chemical. It is a type of **protein** that fights bacteria, fungi, and viruses. The protein spreads throughout the plant, finds the invader, and destroys it.

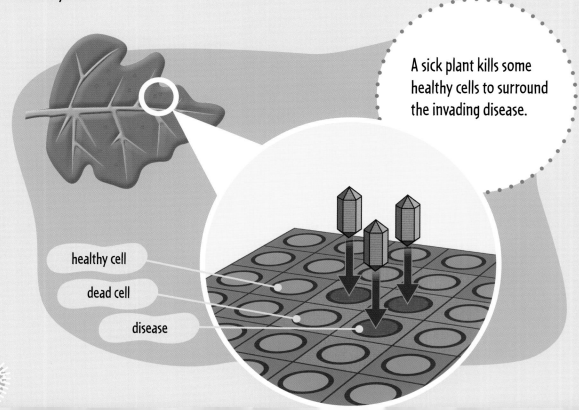

A sick plant kills some healthy cells to surround the invading disease.

healthy cell

dead cell

disease

Plants also protect themselves in another way. They kill the cells surrounding the diseased area to prevent the disease from spreading. This is a recent discovery that may help scientists figure out ways to grow crops that resist disease.

Scientist spotlight: botanists

Botanists are scientists who study plants. Many botanists go on to specialize as plant doctors. They study plants and their diseases and look for ways to cure plants. Many colleges and universities let people bring a sample of their sick plants for a diagnosis. Sometimes the problem is with the plant, but sometimes the problem is in the soil. Botanists figure out the problem and recommend ways to help the plants become healthy again.

A botanist can tell that a fungus has attacked this leaf.

What Is Diabetes?

Your television set and your body both need energy to work. If the electricity goes out in your home, the television stops working. If energy does not reach your body's cells, they, too, stop working. That is what happens with a **disorder** called diabetes.

Energy for human bodies comes from sugar. When we eat food containing **carbohydrates** (candy, soda, pasta, and bread), our bodies break the carbohydrates down into a simple sugar called **glucose**. Within our bodies, a gland called the **pancreas** releases a **hormone** (chemical substance) called **insulin**. Insulin works like a key to unlock the doors into cells and let sugars enter.

For people with diabetes, the pancreas does not make insulin, or it does not make enough insulin to keep cells supplied with glucose. Type 1 diabetes happens when the pancreas does not make insulin at all. People with Type 1 diabetes take insulin shots every day. Type 2 diabetes is when the pancreas makes too little insulin to deliver sugar to cells. People with this form of diabetes may control their diabetes by following a strict diet.

How does diabetes affect cells?

When a person without diabetes eats food, his or her body processes carbohydrates and changes them into glucose. The pancreas makes insulin throughout the day, which lets glucose into the cells. The cells use glucose to get the energy they need.

When a person with diabetes eats food, his or her body also changes the carbohydrates into glucose. But without insulin, the glucose remains in the blood and does not provide energy to the cells.

A diet for someone with diabetes is designed to make the maximum amount of energy reach hungry muscle and organ cells.

The body automatically reacts if it finds too much sugar in the blood. Cells send a message to pass **urine**, because the body is trying to get rid of the extra sugar. Other cells sense the loss of water, and the body gets a message to drink more water. Cells are starved for energy, so the body gets a message to eat more to provide that energy. And when cells cannot get energy from sugar, they rob it from **fats** and **proteins**.

What are the risks?

Diabetes can have serious effects on a person's health. Without medical attention, diabetes takes over the body. **Diabetics** (people with diabetes) can suffer from heart disease and are more likely to die from flu or pneumonia. Their kidneys may become damaged and stop working. In serious cases, diabetics may go into a coma or have serious eye damage and go blind.

Diabetics may need insulin shots or pills. They also need to watch what they eat. Cakes, candy, and sugary drinks put too much sugar directly into the body. Doctors advise diabetics to eat balanced meals with proteins, **complex carbohydrates**, and vegetables. To make sure that blood sugar levels are under control, diabetics test their blood several times a day. It is also important for diabetics to get regular exercise. It helps to regulate blood sugar levels.

With proper meal planning, someone with diabetes can occasionally enjoy a small piece of cake.

Testing blood sugar

The amount of glucose, or sugar, normally found in the blood changes throughout the day. Normally, blood sugar levels vary from as low as 70 milligrams in the morning to as high as 140 milligrams after meals. For diabetics, when first rising in the morning, blood sugar levels may be as low as 50 milligrams. High levels go well beyond 140 milligrams. Diabetics change the amount of insulin they take to even out their blood sugar level.

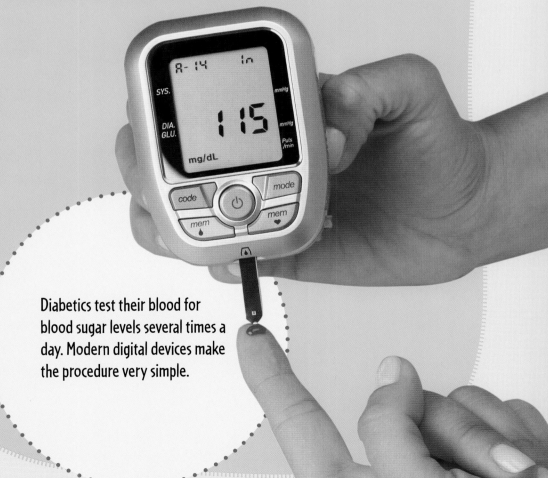

Diabetics test their blood for blood sugar levels several times a day. Modern digital devices make the procedure very simple.

What Is Cancer?

Cancer is a disease that results when abnormal cells begin to reproduce out of control. Cancer cells develop from normal cells that change, which is a process called **mutation**. Many cancer cells form **tumors**, which are clusters of cells that continue to grow. Other cancers affect blood or other body fluids.

There are more than 200 different types of cells in humans. There are also more than 200 different types of cancer. Each different type of cancer affects a different type of human cell.

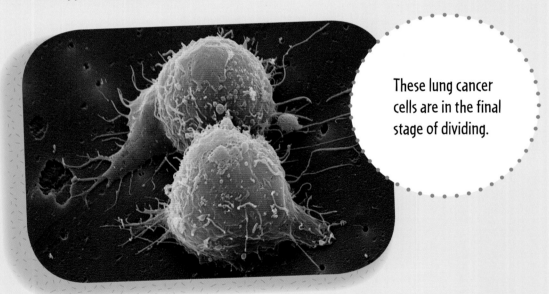

These lung cancer cells are in the final stage of dividing.

How do we test for cancer?

When doctors suspect cancer in a patient, they order tests. For **leukemia** (a cancer of the blood), a blood test is enough. For other cancers, if the patient has a tumor, doctors take a sample of the tumor's cells. This process is called a biopsy. The sample is studied under a microscope, and cancer cells may be identified. Not all tumors lead to cancer.

For other patients, doctors may order an X-ray or MRI (see box at right). This technology allows doctors to see the size, shape, and exact location of tumors deep in the body. MRIs also show if cancer has spread.

How cancer develops

How do cancer cells mutate, or change? A **virus** attacks a normal cell, or a cell comes into contact with cancer-causing agents. Its **DNA** becomes damaged. That abnormal cell reproduces, which creates a new cell with more changes. Abnormal cells go through four changes before they develop into cancer cells. Then, the cancer cells get out of control as they reproduce.

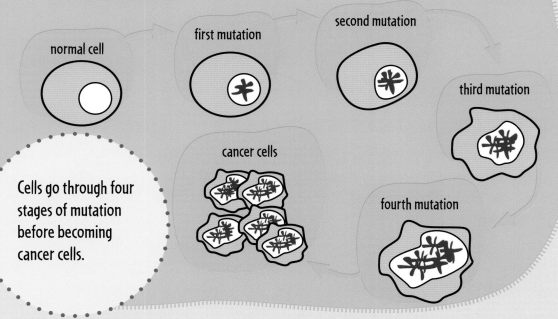

normal cell

first mutation

second mutation

third mutation

fourth mutation

cancer cells

Cells go through four stages of mutation before becoming cancer cells.

Science tools:
magnetic resonance imaging (MRI)

MRI stands for "magnetic resonance imaging." An MRI takes pictures of an area of a body in slices. A computer puts the slices together and produces a three-dimensional picture of the area that was scanned.

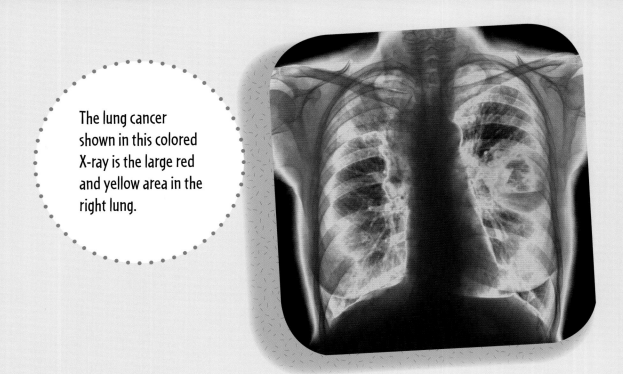

The lung cancer shown in this colored X-ray is the large red and yellow area in the right lung.

Who can get cancer?

Children and adults tend to get different types of cancer. The most common cancers among children are leukemia, brain cancer, and cancer of the nervous system. These three cancers account for more than half of all new children's cancer cases yearly.

For men, the most common cancers are **prostate** (an organ involved in reproduction) cancer, lung cancer, and colorectal cancer (cancer of the colon or rectum). Women tend to get breast cancer, lung cancer, and colorectal cancer.

Hope for the future

Fifty years ago, treatments for cancer were not very successful. Today, cancer treatment combines surgery to remove tumors, chemical therapy (chemotherapy), and **radiation** treatments to kill any remaining cancer cells. Researchers continue to work on better medicines to cure cancer and on **vaccines** that will prevent people from getting cancer.

The problem in finding a cure or a vaccine for cancer is that many different agents cause cancer. Viruses cause some cancers, such as liver and cervical cancer. Skin cancer can result from too much sun. Smoking or breathing in **pollution** may cause lung cancer. A cure for cancer may come one type of cancer at a time.

How Does HIV/AIDS Affect Cells?

HIV stands for "human immunodeficiency virus." This **virus** causes a disease called AIDS (acquired immunodeficiency syndrome).

HIV is transferred from person to person through certain body fluids. People spread the virus through having unprotected sex, sharing drug needles, and, sometimes, when being tattooed with unclean needles. HIV-positive mothers can pass the virus to their unborn children. They may also pass HIV through their milk.

How does HIV spread?

HIV lives in cells and spreads through a person's body fluids. It moves into lung **tissue** and other body parts. The virus becomes part of the victim's cells.

HIV destroys **white blood cells**, the cells that are an important part of the **immune system**. As the number of white blood cells in the body is reduced, the chances of getting sick increase. The virus spreads throughout the body and kills too many white blood cells. Eventually, the person with HIV becomes a victim of AIDS. But it may take 10 years or longer before the victim develops AIDS.

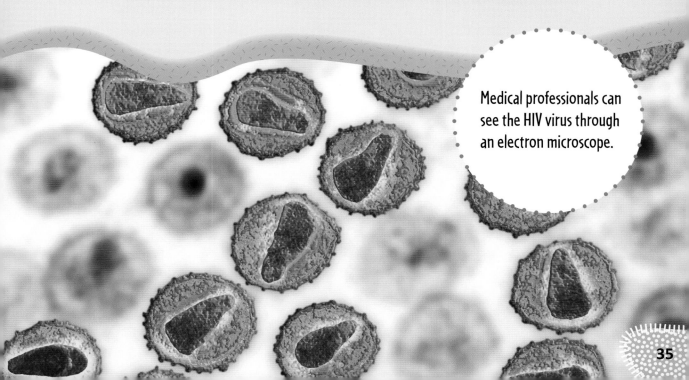

Medical professionals can see the HIV virus through an electron microscope.

How does AIDS affect a body?

When people develop AIDS, they have so few white blood cells that they can no longer fight off disease. **Bacteria**, viruses, and **fungi** invade their bodies. They may feel tired, weak, or have unexplained fevers. They may lose weight quickly or develop skin rashes. Slowly, AIDS victims catch more diseases, and their bodies get weaker. They may die of several different diseases, but they do not actually die of AIDS.

A serious situation

In the last 25 years, the once-unknown disease has quickly become a frightening killer. Today, more than 33 million people live with HIV or AIDS worldwide. The estimated number of deaths due to AIDS globally has exceeded 2 million people yearly since 2003.

Many children in Africa are born with HIV that is passed on from their infected mothers.

So far, scientists have not found a cure for HIV or a **vaccine** to prevent it. They have developed medicines to slow the growth of the virus, but not to destroy the virus. Once a person has HIV, he or she will have the virus and be able to pass it on for life.

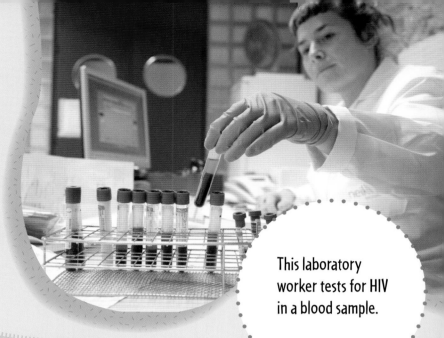

This laboratory worker tests for HIV in a blood sample.

HIV, AIDS, and children

The number of children under age 15 who have HIV and/or AIDS grows constantly. In 2001 about 1.6 million children were HIV positive. By 2008 that number had increased to 2.1 million according to the World Health Organization. More than 90 percent of these children live in Africa south of the Sahara Desert.

ADULTS AND CHILDREN LIVING WITH HIV	
Sub-Saharan Africa	22,400,000
Middle East and North Africa	310,000
South and Southeast Asia	3,800,000
East Asia	850,000
Oceania	59,000
Latin America	2,000,000
Caribbean	240,000
Eastern Europe and Central Asia	1,500,000
Western Europe and Central Europe	850,000
North America	1,400,000

Most children living with HIV/AIDS live in Africa.

Why Are Some People Born With Diseases?

Newborns are tested for possible health problems. What diseases could a newborn possibly have? The answer is in a child's **genes**. **Genetic disorders** are illnesses carried in genes. They may pass from a parent to a child. **Mutations** may also happen when a baby is forming in its mother's womb.

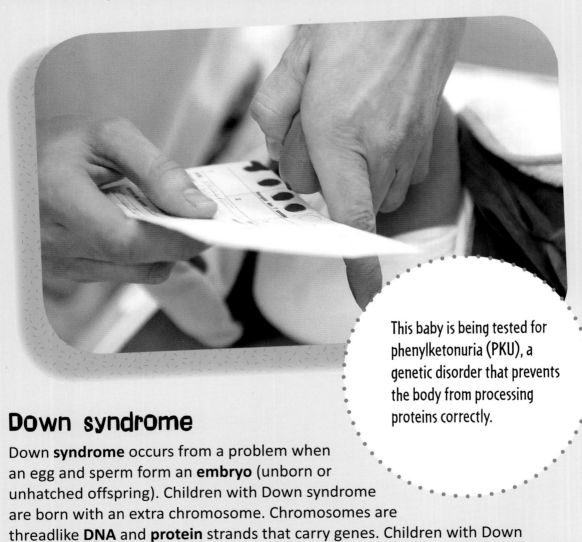

This baby is being tested for phenylketonuria (PKU), a genetic disorder that prevents the body from processing proteins correctly.

Down syndrome

Down **syndrome** occurs from a problem when an egg and sperm form an **embryo** (unborn or unhatched offspring). Children with Down syndrome are born with an extra chromosome. Chromosomes are threadlike **DNA** and **protein** strands that carry genes. Children with Down syndrome may have trouble learning, speaking, seeing, or hearing. Physical and mental disabilities related to Down syndrome vary with each child.

Sickle-cell anemia

Unlike Down syndrome, sickle-cell anemia is passed from parents to children. People with this disease have **red blood cells** that are crescent shaped (or sickle shaped), instead of round like doughnuts. Sickle-shaped cells form clumps and get stuck in veins and **arteries** (vessels carrying blood from the heart). The cells cannot carry oxygen or remove carbon dioxide properly. People with sickle-cell anemia tire easily and have pain in joints and muscles. Both parents must carry the trait (characteristic) for sickle cells for a child to be born with the condition.

Tay-Sachs

Living with Down syndrome or sickle-cell anemia is not always easy, but children born with Tay-Sachs rarely live past five years old. For Tay-Sachs victims, the body does not process **fats** properly. Fats collect in the brain and prevent normal physical and mental development. Both parents must have the mutated gene for their child to have Tay-Sachs.

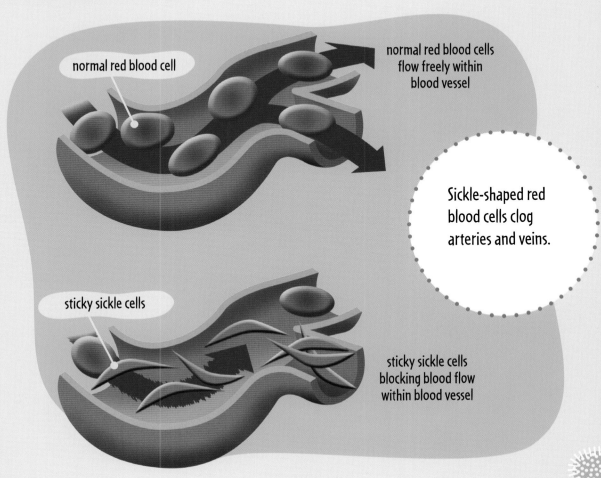

normal red blood cell

normal red blood cells flow freely within blood vessel

Sickle-shaped red blood cells clog arteries and veins.

sticky sickle cells

sticky sickle cells blocking blood flow within blood vessel

Hemophilia

Some genetic disorders are carried by only one parent. Women are carriers of the mutated gene that causes the disease hemophilia, but only men suffer from the disease. Hemophiliacs have blood that does not clot properly. When they get cut, bleeding does not stop quickly. Hemophiliacs must be careful not to get cuts or bruises. These accidents, common to children, might kill a hemophiliac.

Genetic testing

Not all genetic disorders threaten lives. Color blindness prevents a person from seeing the difference between red and green or other colors. Boys are more likely to be color-blind than girls. One in 12 boys is color-blind.

People in groups likely to have certain genetic problems may want to be tested to see if they carry a disorder. They may carry the genetic material for diseases like cystic fibrosis or sickle-cell anemia without being sick. Cystic fibrosis is an **inherited** disease that affects the lungs, intestines, and airways. Even if they are not sick, their genes could pass those problems on to their children.

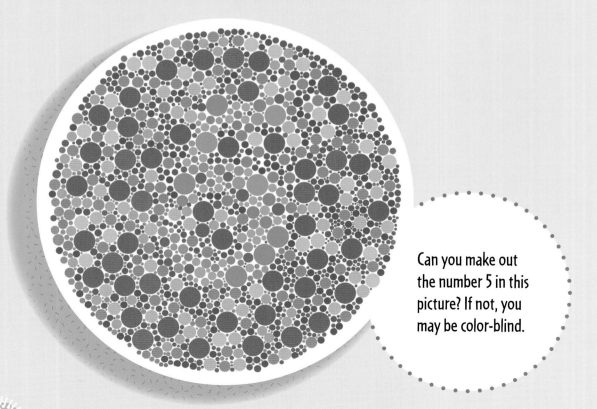

Can you make out the number 5 in this picture? If not, you may be color-blind.

What Are Scientists Doing to Prevent Cell Disorders?

Scientists are trying to find ways to help people handle **genetic disorders**. Better medicines make living with cystic fibrosis or sickle-cell anemia easier. Yet scientists want to stop these disorders from happening. Two ideas that might work are using **stem cells** and changing a person's **genes**.

Stem cells

Stem cells are found in adult humans, blood from an umbilical cord, and in **embryos** less than two weeks old. Stem cells are important because they may become specialized cells such as heart cells, bone cells, skin cells, and so on.

Scientists think that stem cells might cure diabetes, prevent some heart disease, and heal spinal cord injuries. If stem cells can become any human cell, could they be directed to form new lung cells or nerve cells? If so, they might be able to repair damaged lung **tissue** or nerve cells in a spinal cord. Scientists believe that stem cells may be a breakthrough in repairing damaged bodies.

The problem is that the most positive results come from using stem cells from embryos. Some people are worried that scientists may produce human embryos purely for doing experiments.

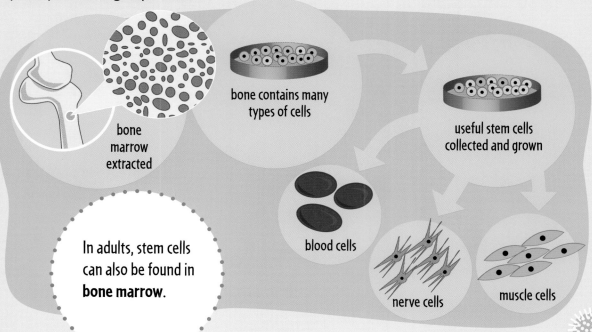

bone marrow extracted

bone contains many types of cells

useful stem cells collected and grown

blood cells

nerve cells

muscle cells

In adults, stem cells can also be found in **bone marrow**.

How to find out if you carry genetic disorders

Other interesting studies involve genetic testing and gene therapy. Genetic testing discovers if someone carries a gene for a genetic disease. Tests are available for many diseases such as Tay-Sachs and hemophilia. Scientists are working on tests for other genetic disorders. Knowing that their children might develop genetic disorders gives adults choices. Parents might choose to adopt a child rather than risk having a child born with Tay-Sachs, for example.

Genetic testing can also determine if a person is more likely to get a disease than other people. For example, some women are more likely to get breast cancer than others. In this case, the woman would get screened for breast cancer frequently. Testing and screening could save a life.

Can stem cells one day help some wheelchair-bound people to walk again?

Gene therapy

Going a step further, scientists hope to repair damaged genes so that children will not be born with some genetic disorders. This process is called gene therapy. Scientists hope to identify genetic problems early and repair damaged genes in an embryo.

Doctors may test patients before they have children to see if the patients have a genetic disorder that might be passed on to a baby.

Some people do not agree that scientists should try to correct these problems. They may have religious, legal, or moral objections to gene repair therapy.

However, 500 years ago, people regularly died of the **plague** or smallpox. One hundred years ago, many children died from measles or were **paralyzed** by polio. Science found answers to those diseases. What is the next great medical advancement? It may be a **vaccine** to prevent all cancers, or a fix for damaged spinal cords. No one knows. Only by studying disease at the cellular level can scientists find the answers to today's health problems.

Glossary

antibiotic medicine that destroys bacteria

agent something that produces an effect; in this case disease

artery blood vessel that carries blood away from the heart

bacterium (plural: bacteria) a single-celled microscopic living organism

bone marrow substance inside bones that produces blood cells

carbohydrate sugar or starch

complex carbohydrate starch or sugar that provides long-term energy for an animal's body

deoxyribonucleic acid (DNA) nucleic acids that carry the traits and characteristics of a living thing

diabetic person who has diabetes

diarrhea liquid or runny feces

disorder condition of unusual or disrupted body function

embryo unborn or unhatched offspring of an animal

fat naturally occurring greasy or waxy substance

feces solid animal waste

fungus a spore-producing organism; can cause infections

gene blueprint for a living thing, made of DNA

genetic relating to genes or inherited characteristics

glucose simple sugar

hormone chemical substance produced in animal bodies

host site for disease to take hold

immune resistant to a particular infection

immune system parts in a body that fight disease or infection

infection presence of bacteria, virus, or another agent that causes disease

inherited passed down from parent to child

insulin chemical substance that allows the body to process sugar

leukemia cancer of the blood

lymph colorless liquid containing white blood cells

microorganism extremely small living thing

mineral necessary substance like calcium or iron that comes from food, but is made of inorganic material

mucus slimy substance produced in the body for protection of delicate tissues

mutation change in a gene

node tissue mass

nutrient substance in food that helps growth and health

organism living thing

pancreas gland that produces insulin

paralysis inability to move one's muscles

parasite foreign organism that must live on or in another organism

plague bacterial infection that often causes death

pollution presence or introduction of harmful substances

prostate organ in male mammals that produces the liquid in which sperm are carried

protein molecule found in the body that builds muscles, bones, hair, and nails and is made up of amino acids

protist single-celled organism

radiation particles of energy that cause changes in cell structures

red blood cell cell in animal blood that carries oxygen through the body

ribonucleic acid (RNA) nucleic acid in cells that chooses genes and sends messages to cells about what they should do

stem cell general or basic cell that can develop into more specific cells

symptom something felt by an infected person that often cannot be measured by a doctor, such as a headache

syndrome signs and symptoms that are grouped together to describe a physical condition

tissue two or more types of cells that work together to perform a specific job

tumor irregular tissue formation in a plant or animal

urine liquid animal waste

vaccine substance that builds antibodies to prevent disease

vector agent that carries disease

virus protein molecule that bonds with cells and causes disease

vomit matter ejected from the stomach through the mouth

white blood cell part of blood that fights infection and disease

Find Out More

Books to read

Allman, Toney. *Stem Cell Research*. Yankton, S.D.: Erickson, 2007.

Cregan, Elizabeth R. *Pioneers in Cell Biology*. Mankato, Minn.: Compass Point, 2010.

Fridell, Ron. *Genetic Engineering*. Minneapolis: Lerner, 2006.

Goldsmith, Connie. *Superbugs Strike Back: When Antibiotics Fail*. Minneapolis: Twenty-First Century, 2007.

Lee, Kimberly Fekany. *Cell Scientists from Leeuwenhoek to Fuchs*. Mankato, Minn.: Compass Point, 2009.

Margulies, Phillip. *Down Syndrome*. New York: Rosen, 2007.

Peak, Lizabeth. *Sickle Cell Disease*. San Diego: Lucent, 2008.

Powell, Jillian. *Explaining Cystic Fibrosis*. Mankato, Minn.: Smart Apple Media, 2009.

Simons, Rae. *AIDS & HIV: The Facts for Kids*. Vestal, N.Y.: AlphaHouse, 2009.

Siy, Alexandra. *Sneeze!* Watertown, Mass.: Charlesbridge, 2007.

Walker, Julie. *Tay-Sachs Disease*. New York: Rosen, 2007.

Websites

"KidsHealth"
http://kidshealth.org
This website talks about every aspect of health for kids and teens.

"Kids Cancer Network"
www.kidscancernetwork.org
Learn more about cancer and how it affects children.

"Children and HIV"
www.hivinfosource.org/hivis/hivbasics/children
Get the facts about HIV and AIDS and how it affects children.

"The Stem Cell Story"
http://kids.jdrf.org/index.cfm?fuseaction=home.viewpage&page_
id=938B773C-5004-D739-A5CFDCC492B34528
Learn about the research being done with stem cells to find a cure for diabetes.

"Disorder Zone Archives"
www.specialchild.com/disorder.html
Many medical disorders that affect children are linked to genetics. Learn more about these diseases at this website.

"Living with Diabetes: For Parents and Kids"
www.diabetes.org/living-with-diabetes/parents-and-kids
Diabetes is common and may affect you, your family, or your friends. Learn about diabetes and what you can do to help people you know with this disease.

Become an expert

- Make a chart of viral diseases and their signs and symptoms. Draw a conclusion about how viruses affect the body.

- Make a timeline of advances in vaccinations. Note how many of the diseases for which vaccines have been developed are no longer problems in our lives.

- Investigate allergies. How do allergies affect cells? Why are some people allergic to peanuts, while other people are allergic to pet hair, pollen, or other substances? What are common signs and symptoms of allergies?

- Learn more about genetic disorders. Find one genetic disorder that interests you and write a report about it.

Index